Biophilia

Chrissie Petrie

I dedicate this book to Tony and my Mam & Dad.

For all of your support and encouragement, I am truly grateful.

Thank you

x

CONTENTS

Pulitzer prize winning biologist Edward Wilson coined the term biophilia, a deep need to connect with nature.

This is a collection of short syllabic poems, each a berry to burst on the readers' lips, plucked freshly from nature and preserved within these pages, with the hope that they will instill a sense of biophilia in everyone.

'There is a pleasure in the pathless woods
There is a rapture on the lonely shore
There is society, where none intrudes
By the deep sea, and music in its roar
I love not man less, but nature more'

Lord Byron
Childe Harold's Pilgrimage
CLXXVIII

SPRING

The grey membrane peels
away like a cling-film wrap
to reveal vibrant
blues, yellows and greens in a
coastal countryside painting

A cloud
morphs through the sky
...a panther...a gecko...
a compass needle pointing north
...a cloud

The bird road re-opens

Blue tits and finches
decorate the bare bushes
like misplaced baubles

Chrissie Petrie

Bright
bugles beam
from grassy banks

Feathered darts rest needle-deep in soil

Soft
wings waft
in warming winds

An old retriever, all fat and fur,
leaps, lands, slap down centre in the water.
His tail swishes and sludge sloshes as he splashes
with the zeal of a playful pup

From
tight fists,
leafy fingers fan

A
leaf cranes
towards the
floor, like a swan
stooping to see its
reflection. The tip hangs
an inch from the ground. There are
other leaves around but none are
touching. In the centre of this one
leaf a snail sits, stretches its neck to snack

Statuesque kestrel
scanning silently for prey
poised on a fence post

The pit pond swells with jelly balls
Black eyes bulging in the pulsing mass

Long faces lean low,
inviting bites from barbed teeth,
to taste the sweet green stalks
from the field beyond the fence

Barbs nest in tufts of
coarse hair where a
tangled tail, tugged through
tightly wound wire, flicks

Orange
shards splinter
the dark sky

A hollow hermit shell lays
lightly upon caramel
sands where sea-soaked stones fizzle
like Cava over ice-cubes

SUMMER

A silver pot steams
on a mosaic bistro top.
Aromas of rich
Arabica drift up as
the sun kisses ears of wheat.

Tongues lick
Teeth tug
Tails flick
Hides shrug

A peck of naughty pixies
lay bare on their backs
amongst the leaves
in the shade of the trees

A low rumbling gives short warning
of a heavy downpour but the
birds remain merry and a
duo of young deer
keep on grazing in
an opening
at the edge
of the
dene

As
   the
 rain-
drops
     stop
 the
     fields
pop
    pop
pop!

Tiny olive toads,
pinkie nail small, give
faint pulses to
the windless rushes

Sticky thick and still,
it drapes the
open windowsill

Early evening breeze
fragranced with the sweet scent of
warm wax and honey

Fuzz like the
fizz of warm
ginger ale

Her lustring wings tickle
the mellifluous lips of
Zephyr. She cha-chas.
Seduces Myositis,
Narcissus, Anemone.
Tongues liquid sun

Purple thistles
bristle with the
bustle of bees

Under summer moon
the spider spins her silver
dream catcher of death

As
black
as the
ambient
night, they flap their crepe
wings like bunting in the warm wind

Sagging
sky splits,
quenches parched earth

Each day it grows smaller.
The smell of onions stronger.
More flies gather around
fox prints in the clay.

The world has been erased. All
that remains is a grey page
with a faint etching of a
line here and a smudge there

AUTUMN

Where tractor tracks cut through clods
of mud and severed rapeseed
stalks, sparrows, pigeons and crows
take their lunch sittings in
ascending order of size

A family of
plump pheasants feasting in a
freshly turned field

The ground blushes
as stripped trees flirt with
winter's wooing wind

On Beacon Hill
a curl-billed curlew probes the
mist moist soil

The North Sea serenades the land
under a low lit slip of a moon

The world is a tangle of webs.
Each delicate weave decorated with translucent jewels.

Worn
weathered
strips, stretched the
width of a trunk,
paint an aged face in dirty bandages

A leech,   ripples over
        like a liquorice whip,   dappled sand

Black orange, mimicking
brick, they hang on fine
strings like earrings

The flutter of a
feather snagged on a branch. The
scratch of paws below.
A nose wrinkles, sniffs the air,
retreats through the undergrowth.

Periwinkle
sky reflects
mirror glass sea

Witches broomsticks twitch in the mist

Swirl, swoop. Wingspan. Tail fan. Flick,
dip, dive. The hunter now the
hunted as the sparrow hawk
leads and the crow mocks behind

Low clouds surge
through the pale sky like
a phantom army

A silver fly with
red eyes hides in the
hole of a wooden door
in a rundown yard

Red rivulets course
down cracks in
old farm tracks

WINTER

Two red breasts settle
on a wall.
Winter's messengers.

Sky pillow rips
Soft feathers flutter
Muffle the earth

A
single
berry blood-
spots the
branch

The silk sea wrinkles

A spruce sprig skims thin ice

Stars spark down
a dark sky like needles
through black satin

A bare bough wears its heart for all to see

The winter sun falls on hedgerow's ossified fingers.
Light shards splice ivy's webbed hands.

A yellow fleck flits
from brush to shrub. A wink of
sun and whoosh! it's gone.

Sparrows spray water
as they bathe
in the melted snow

Winter clings with
brittle fingers, tip deep
in puddles, nails
scraping on fallen leaves

A fountain of flies
effervesce, luminous in
the light of the sun,
hypnotic, like the tick tock
of a swaying pendulum.

Clover grows on mounds where moles once burrowed

Heads hang in
woodland beds, bright
as lightning bolts.

Fine
feathers,
like flags on
Everest, mark
shards of shells polished clean by orange beaks.

A
squadron
of geese fly
in formation,
every flap of each wing heralding spring.

Since graduating from university with a Masters Degree in Creative Writing, Chrissie Petrie has seen her work published in anthologies in the UK, USA and Asia. She has won several competitions and has been shortlisted in numerous others. Chrissie also works as a creative practitioner, designing and delivering creative writing workshops and projects within schools and community groups. For more information you can visit her website using the following link:

http://chrissiepetrie.wordpress.com/